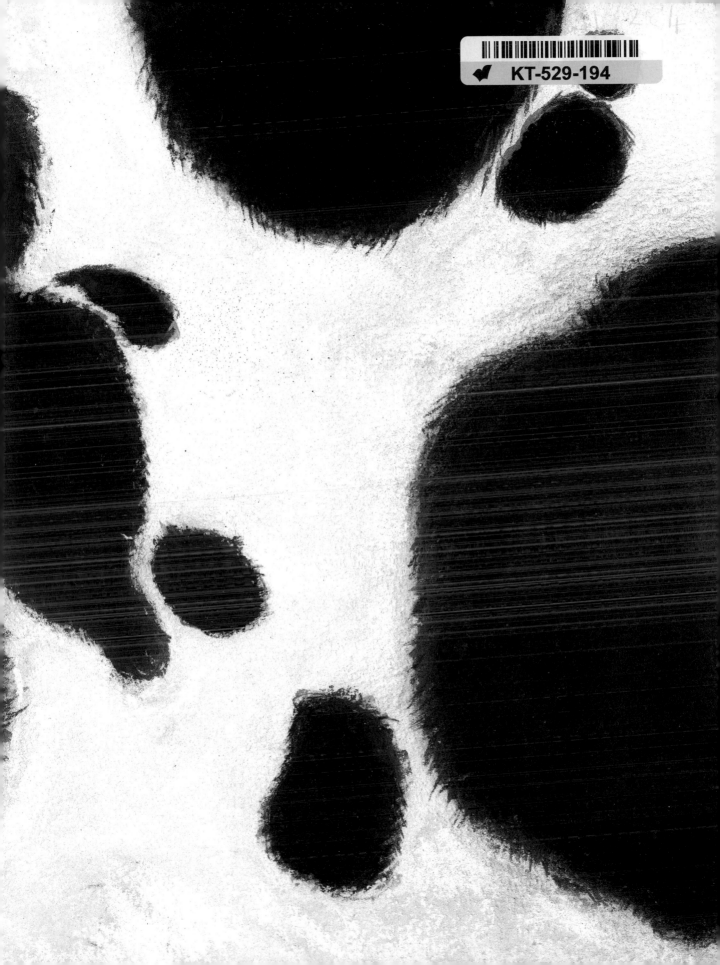

Animal Rhymes

Compiled by John Foster

Illustrated by Carol Thompson

Oxford University Press

Oxford   New York   Toronto

Oxford University Press, Great Clarendon Street, Oxford OX2 6DP

Oxford   New York
Athens Auckland Bangkok Bogota Bombay
Buenos Aires Calcutta Cape Town Dar es Salaam
Delhi Florence Hong Kong Istanbul Karachi
Kuala Lumpur Madras Madrid Melbourne
Mexico City Nairobi Paris Singapore
Taipei Tokyo Toronto Warsaw

and associated companies in
Berlin   Ibadan

Oxford is a trade mark of Oxford University Press

This selection and arrangement © John Foster 1998
Illustrations © Carol Thompson 1998
First published 1998

John Foster and Carol Thompson have asserted their moral
right to be identified as the authors of this work.

A CIP catalogue record for this book is available
from the British Library

ISBN 0 19 276164 1 (paperback)
ISBN 0 19 276204 4 (hardback)

Printed in Belgium

Contents

Scuttle Like a Crab

Scuttle like a crab. Creep like a snail. Swim like a dolphin. Dive like a whale.

Stalk like a lion. Pounce like a cat. Jump like a kangaroo. Run like a rat.

Wriggle like a worm. Hop like a frog. Wag your tail and pant like a dog!

John Foster

Archibald the Spider

Spin spin spinning
Web across the air,
Archibald the spider
Scuttles here and there.

Don't move a muscle:
That's what counts.
Archibald the spider
Waiting to pounce.

Here comes a visitor.
Can't afford to miss.
Archibald the spider
Leaps like . . . THIS!

Paul Rogers

Little Miss Myrtle

Little Miss Myrtle sat on a turtle,
Thinking that it was a chair;
'Oww eee!' cried the turtle,
'I'm sorry,' said Myrtle,
'I didn't know you were there.'

Carolyn Graham

A Kangaroo

A kangaroo
One afternoon
Jumped so high
It jumped over the moon!

It jumped so far
It jumped so high
It bumped its head
Upon the sky.

Down it fell
Spinning round
And bumped its bottom
On the ground.

Julie Holder

I'm a Giraffe

I'm a giraffe,
with my head in the sky;
watch me stretch my neck up high.

I'm a kangaroo,
with my legs so strong;
watch me as I bounce along.

I'm a chimpanzee,
with my hands down low;
swinging my arms wherever I go.

12

I'm a snake,
with my body on the ground;
watch me as I slither around.

I'm a rabbit,
with my ears that flop;
everybody knows how to bunny hop.

I'm a crocodile,
with my jaws open wide;
why don't you come and look inside?

Mike Jubb

13

Elephant Antics

One little elephant
sitting on a bunk.
Along came another one
and pulled his trunk!

Two little elephants
in a tug-of-war.
Two more joined in
and then there were four.

Four *more* came along,
so there were eight
pulling and tugging
with all their weight.

They all fell over.
And guess what happened then.
They jumped up
and started all over again.

Jill Townsend

14

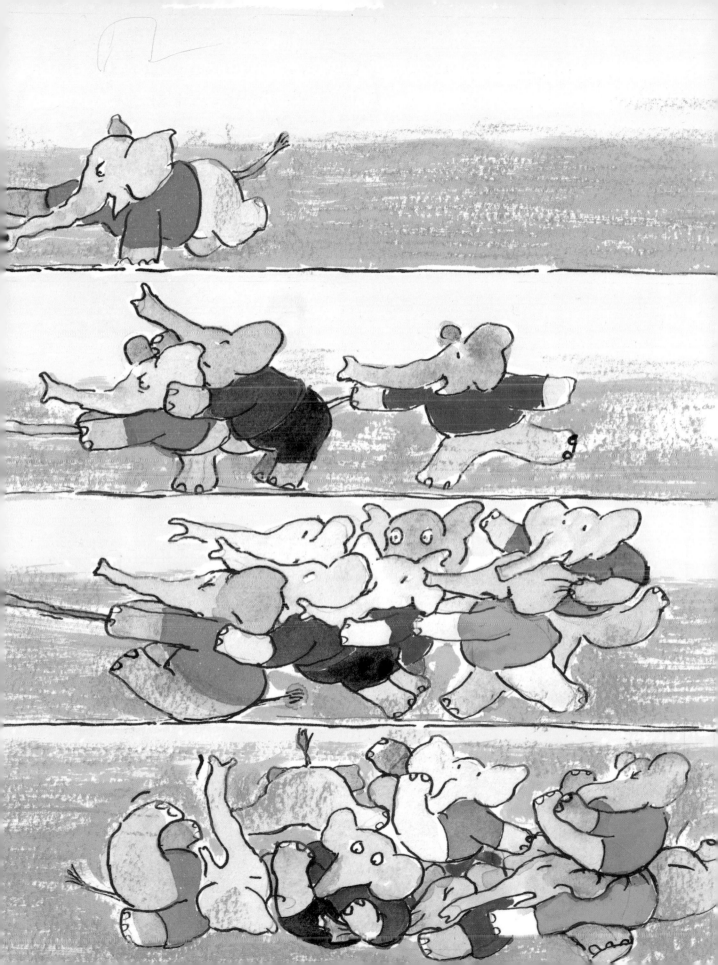

Ducks on the Water

Ducks on the water,
    quack,
    quack,
    quack!
Sailing down the river
And then sailing back.

Mother duck leads,
Ducklings behind,
Trim little swimmers
    in
    a
    long
    straight
    line.

Out of the river,
Into the nest.
Time for the family
To have a rest.

18

Under her wings
Mother duck tucks
Two little drakes
        and
Three little ducks.

Jack Ousbey

Hamish the Hamster

There's a scrabble and a scratch.
There's a scuffle and a squeal.
It's Hamish the Hamster
On his exercise wheel.

There's a nibble and a gnaw.
There's a crackle and a crunch.
It's hungry Hamish Hamster
Chewing up his lunch.

Tony Mitton

My Goldfish

My goldfish is the perfect pet.
She isn't any trouble.
She doesn't bark,
She doesn't mew,
    just bubble
        bubble
          bubbles.

My goldfish is the perfect pet.
She isn't any trouble.
We don't have to feed her much,
She doesn't need a rabbit hutch,
    just bubble
        bubble
          bubbles.

Marie Brookes

21

One Little Sparrow

One little sparrow
Pecking at the crumbs.
One beak pecking,
Then another comes.

Two little sparrows
Pecking at the crumbs.
Two beaks pecking,
Then another comes.

Three little sparrows
Pecking at the crumbs.
Three beaks pecking,
Then a pussy comes.

22

No little sparrows
Pecking at the crumbs.
Sparrows don't like pussies—
They fly off to their mums.

One little pussy cat.
Now there are two.
Now there's a third one
Coming into view.

Three little pussy cats,
Soon there'll be none.
A doggy comes and barks.
Away they all run.

Clive Webster

The Egg Song

Peck, peck, peck,
went the little chick's beak.
Out poked its head
as it took a little peek.

Out stepped its leg.
Out flapped its wing.
Then the fluffy yellow chick
began to sing:

'Take me to the water.
Show me to the seed.
If I'm going to live and grow,
that is what I'll need.

'Then when I'm a chicken,
feathery and grown,
I can cluck and lay an egg
all of my own.'

Tony Mitton

The Cuckoo Calls

The cuckoo calls, coo, coo, coo,
Don't touch the mangoes any of you,
For I am the mango queen you see,
Eating mangoes is for me.

Traditional Indian

A Nature Walk

One for the rabbit who nibbled the hay.
Two for the field-mice who scuttled away.
Three for the weasels with beady black eyes.
Four for the frogs in the pond catching flies.
Five for the foxes with fine bushy tails.
Six for the slugs with their silvery trails.
Seven for the skylarks who sang in the sky.
Eight for the squirrels who scampered by.
Nine for the hedgehogs who shuffled around.
Ten for the badgers who hid underground.

Marian Swinger

Farmyard Count

One for a baa
Two for a moo
Three for a flap and a cock-a-doodle-doo
Four for an oink
Five for hee-haw
Six for a squeak and a rustle in the straw
Seven for a neigh
Eight for a bark
Nine for a hoot in the barn roof dark
Ten for a quack
Eleven for meow
Twelve for the farmyard
ALL TOGETHER NOW! . . .

Julie Holder

We are grateful to the following for permission to publish their poems for the first time in this collection:

John Foster: 'Scuttle Like a Crab', Copyright © John Foster 1998. **Carolyn Graham:** 'I Saw a Rabbit', Copyright © Carolyn Graham 1998. **Julie Holder:** 'A Kangaroo' and 'Farmyard Count', both Copyright © Julie Holder 1998. **Mike Jubb:** 'I'm a Giraffe', Copyright © Mike Jubb 1998. **Paul Rogers:** 'Archibald the Spider', Copyright © Paul Rogers 1998. **Marian Swinger:** 'A Nature Walk', Copyright © Marian Swinger 1998. **Jill Townsend:** 'Elephant Antics', Copyright © Jill Townsend 1998. **Clive Webster:** 'One Little Sparrow', Copyright © Clive Webster 1998.

We also acknowledge permission to include previously published poems:

Marie Brookes: 'My Goldfish', Copyright © Marie Brookes 1991, first published in *Pet Poems* (Oxford Reading Tree), reprinted by permission of the author. **Carolyn Graham:** 'Little Miss Myrtle', Copyright © Carolyn Graham 1994, first published in *Mother Goose Jazz Chants* (OUP, New York, 1994), reprinted by permission of the author. **Tony Mitton:** 'Hamish the Hamster', first published on 'Pets' poster for Scholastic Infants Projects, and 'The Egg Song', first published in *Child Education* magazine (Scholastic), both Copyright © Tony Mitton, reprinted here by permission of the author. **Jack Ousbey:** 'Ducks on the Water', first published in *Tots TV* magazine (Fleetway, 1994), Copyright © Jack Ousbey 1994, reprinted here by permission of the author.

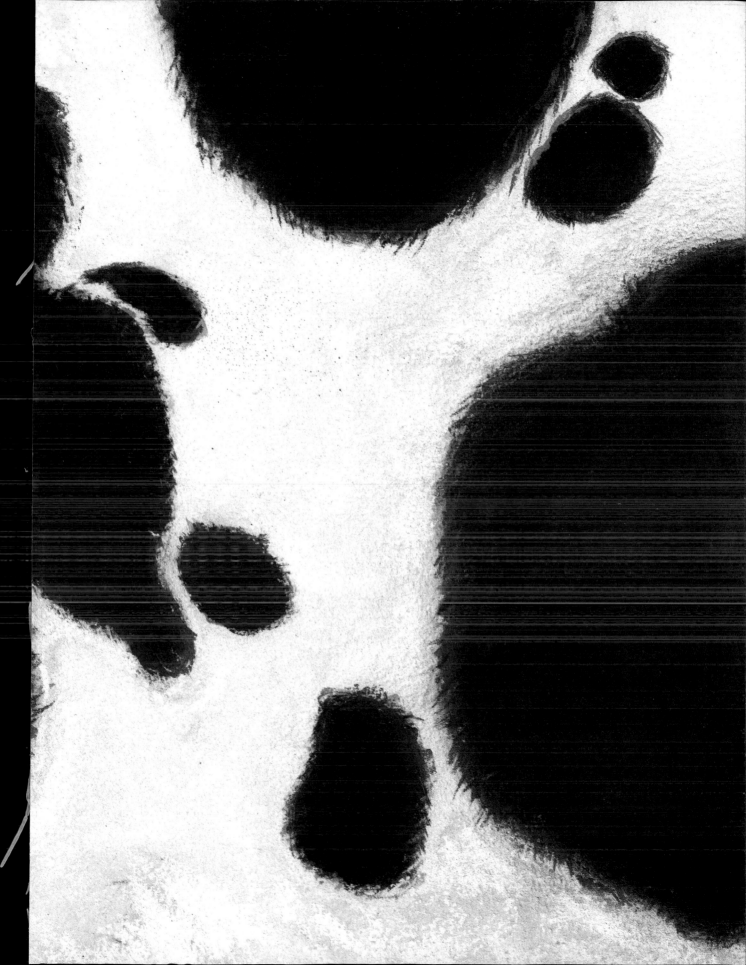

BRIEF CONTENTS